VEGETABLE
GARDENING
WISDOM

VEGETABLE GARDENING WISDOM

Daily Advice and Inspiration for Getting the Most from Your Garden

KELLY SMITH TRIMBLE

Storey Publishing

For Derek

Your support helps me grow through every season.

◇◇◇

The mission of Storey Publishing is to serve our customers by publishing practical information that encourages personal independence in harmony with the environment.

Edited by Carleen Madigan, Hannah Fries, and Corey Cusson
Art direction and book design by Jeff Stiefel and Ash Austin
Text production by Erin Dawson
Indexed by Christine R. Lindemer, Boston Road Communications
Illustrations by © Harriet Popham

Storey books are available for special premium and promotional uses and for customized editions. For further information, please call 800-793-9396.

Storey Publishing
210 MASS MoCA Way
North Adams, MA 01247
storey.com

Printed in China by R.R. Donnelley
10 9 8 7 6 5 4 3 2 1

Library of Congress Cataloging-in-Publication Data on file

GROW YOUR INNER
GARDENER

◇◇◇◇◇◇◇◇◇◇◇◇◇◇◇◇◇◇

I grew up in a small town in eastern Tennessee, and though my family didn't grow our food, we were connected with those who did. One of my favorite weekly errands was stopping in the Ripe 'n' Ready, a farmer's co-op with rows of simple wooden bins filled with fresh vegetables and nuts, shelves of local honey and milk, and barrels of homemade jelly candies. Every summer, we'd load up paper bags with greens beans and sit on the front porch to string them. My mother and grandmother would make a pot of beans (cooked with ham and served with cornbread, of course) and then can the leftovers. It sounds idyllic and, looking back, it was.

*I believe that you, too, can grow
at least some of what you eat, no matter
where you live and regardless of what else
is requiring your time and attention.*

I took that sense of small-town connection with me to college, where I studied environmental ethics. When I was a senior, I went with one of my classes to visit a beautiful family farm tucked inside a cove beneath the Cumberland Plateau in middle Tennessee. I learned about rotational grazing, stood in awe of the fields of vegetables, saw cultivated mushrooms for the first time, and fell in love with the farm's deep connection to the land.

That experience showed me that growing food could be a deeply personal and satisfying way of connecting with and protecting the environment. As Wendell Berry in his essay "Think Little" writes: "I can think of no better form of personal involvement in the cure of the environment than that of gardening. A person who is growing a garden, if he is growing it organically, is improving a piece of the world."

In my cubicle at my first publishing job, in Birmingham, Alabama, I pinned up a photo I'd taken that day at the farm, hoping that I'd one day work my way back to that rural ideal. But what I've discovered over the past 15 years or more of gardening is that the backyard garden (or front yard, if that's where your sun is) offers more opportunities than I'd ever imagined.

It *is* possible for anyone to grow their own food, at least some of it; you don't have to live in a small town or picturesque landscape. I've done it — at my third-floor urban apartment, where I planted tomatoes in pots in the parking area; at my first house, where I dug up the front yard to try growing a little of everything; and in my suburban backyard, where I currently garden in a series of raised beds.

The key is to start small and think of gardening as a lifelong education. Daily practice is essential to this education — in a practical sense, for more bounty, and in a deeper sense, for developing a connection with the garden as a tool for self-discovery and satisfaction. I know that your attention is likely divided among work, school, family, health, and other responsibilities. Mine is too. That's why I wanted to create a book that

presents bite-sized, seasonally appropriate advice and information that you can take action on immediately or recall when the opportunity arises. If your mind is scattered on a daily basis to the degree that recollection doesn't come easy, flag the pages you're most interested in, and I promise, over time, gardening will help focus your mind. You may even become like me and have to force yourself to think about anything else!

I've organized this book generally by season, from late winter, when days start stretching and the ground wakes up from winter slumber, to late fall, when gardeners start thinking about what can overwinter (kale! parsnips!) and putting the rest to bed. Precise timing, from frost dates to planting times, varies depending on where you live, of course. Topics covered include organic gardening basics, like soil building and planting for pollinators; understanding, choosing, planting, and saving seed; growing in all seasons, climates, and spaces large and small; easy ideas for harvesting, cooking, and preserving produce; and much more.

You will also find quotes from wise gardeners and cooks that are meant to nourish your hunger for connection with the ground and with your food. A common theme among these voices: Know you won't be perfect, but if you truly care about your plants, you will be a good gardener. That's something I've known to be true but had trouble expressing, so I was glad to read it so clearly in the words of Eliot Coleman in *The New Organic Grower*: "Quality is the result of the skill of the producer coupled with care. Experience will provide the skills, but caring must come from within."

For me, growing food has become not only a healthy way to connect with the land and what's on my plate but also a means of meditation. My appreciation for the many acts of gardening has made me more mindful of how all food is grown, prepared, and wasted (or not). It may be helpful for you, too, to think of small acts in the garden, such as planting seeds or pulling weeds, as a mindfulness practice akin to yoga and meditation.

Like making art or turning wood, planting and tending a garden — making compost, starting seeds, observing and identifying insects, and, yes, stringing the green beans — is really a series of small acts that add up to a lifestyle, and a life. My hope is that you will use this book to help guide you in a daily practice as you learn to grow your own food, eat what you grow, and develop a lifelong love of gardening.

LATE WINTER
PLANNING &
SEED-STARTING

◇◇◇◇◇◇◇◇◇◇◇◇◇◇

After holidays and hibernation, I find myself with a deep yearning for green things. Seed catalogs spark my anticipation, and I begin plotting, making new resolutions for the year's garden, always vowing to try a few new plants, techniques, and recipes. This time is as much about devouring gardening wisdom as it is about enjoying the few precious plants we can grow.

For gardeners, the arrival of
mail-order seed catalogs signals the point
when winter turns toward spring.
Sign up for a few and experience this joy for yourself.
Look for seed companies that focus
on varieties for your region.

"

I have seen women
look at jewelry ads with
a misty eye and one hand
resting on the heart,
and I only know
what they're feeling
because that's how
I read the seed catalogs
in January.

Barbara Kingsolver,
Animal, Vegetable, Miracle

If there's a "Ready, Set, Go"
for the gardening season,
it's the last frost date.
An estimation of the date when
you can expect the final frost of the
spring to occur, the last frost
date varies from place to place.
Mark yours on the calendar
and start planning —
the anticipation can get you through
the late winter blues.

Save wood ash

from your fireplace, fire pit, or woodstove to use as a soil amendment. Ash contributes potassium, phosphorus, calcium, and other nutrients. It's also very alkaline, so it can raise soil pH.

thyme   sage   basil   rosemary   cilantro

YOU CAN GROW HERBS year round indoors near a sunny window. Use containers with drainage holes placed on saucers so you don't damage a sill or table. Rosemary, oregano, basil, and sage thrive in the sunniest spots (six hours of exposure a day is ideal), but you can get away with mint, parsley, cilantro, and chives in lower-light conditions.

HERB BUTTER

This is a simple way to feel fancy without spending a lot of money or effort. Choose herbs based on what's in season, and use the butter as a spread or topping, or to infuse baked goods with subtle herbal flavor.

1. Soften 1 stick (½ cup) of unsalted butter in a bowl.

2. Add chopped fresh herbs, such as sage, rosemary, thyme, cilantro, or oregano. Adjust the amount from 2 to 5 tablespoons depending on the potency you desire.

3. Combine the butter, herbs, and a dash of salt by hand with a spoon or spatula.

4. Store in the refrigerator for up to 10 days, or wrap in parchment or wax paper and freeze.

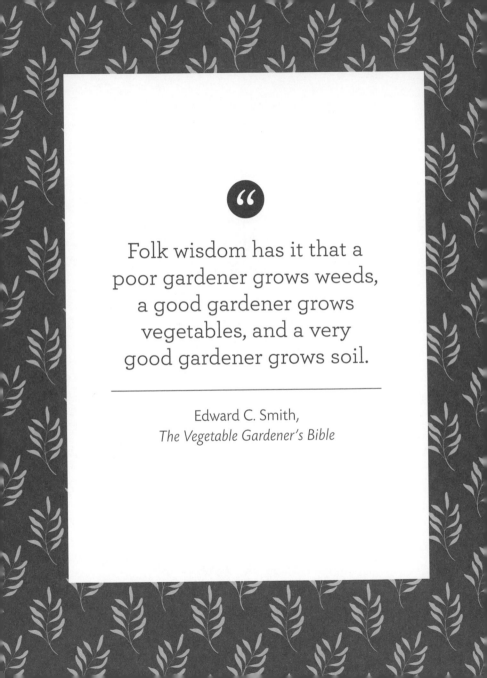

> Folk wisdom has it that a poor gardener grows weeds, a good gardener grows vegetables, and a very good gardener grows soil.

Edward C. Smith,
The Vegetable Gardener's Bible

Think of soil as a living being that needs food, water, and care like we all do. Compost provides food for earthworms and microbes, mulch gives protection against moisture loss, and not walking on or overworking your soil helps it thrive and grow.

Deeper soil is better. Whether you want to grow them in the ground, a raised bed, or a container, most vegetables need to be planted in at least 8 inches of loose soil. Anything less will stunt growth, and anything more will increase it.

CROP ROTATION is the practice of moving crops around the garden, largely by plant family, to avoid common pests and diseases and to account for what certain plants give to or take from the soil. It can get a bit complicated.

FOR SMALL GARDENS, think about dividing vegetables into these groups: legumes (beans and peas), roots, fruiting plants, and leafy greens, and rotate these crops around your garden from year to year.

Treated wood isn't ideal
for building raised beds.
The chemicals that make it
rot resistant can leach
into surrounding soil and
affect soil microbes.
Cedarwood naturally repels
pests and, though pricey,
is a better bet for long-term
soil health.

Make your raised beds

no wider than twice your arm's length.

You should be able to reach

the center to harvest without straining.

A 4 x 4-foot block

is a good size to start with.

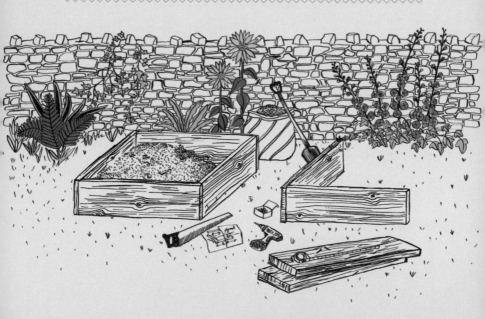

> How large the garden should be is often hastily decided when the gardener is in the flush of spring fever. That's a bad time! It's like going grocery shopping when you're hungry.

Mel Bartholomew,
Square Foot Gardening

Consider day length when choosing onion varieties. Short-day varieties will produce bulbs better in the South, where they get closer to equal amounts of light and dark. Long-day varieties are best in the North, where there are more hours of light in summer. Day-neutral varieties do well anywhere.

LONG SUMMER DAYS —
with up to 20 hours of sunlight —
help gardeners in Alaska
grow off-the-charts-big vegetables,
like cabbages and pumpkins.
That increased photosynthesis
also makes the veggies sweeter.
It's a nice prize for those with
such a short growing season —
only about four months from
last frost to first.

Phenology, the study of weather and
its effect on plant and animal cycles,
looks at climate signs rather than a calendar
to determine planting and harvest dates.
For example, phenological wisdom suggests
sowing beets and carrots when
dandelions start to bloom and planting
potatoes as the daffodils flower.

INDOOR SPROUTS

You can have a steady supply of homegrown greens even in the depths of winter by growing sprouts indoors. Use a jar with a mesh or perforated lid for draining.

1. Drop a spoonful of sprouting seeds, like alfalfa, radish, chickpea, or lentil, into the jar and cover with water.

2. Soak overnight, then drain.

3. Rinse and drain daily until sprouts fill the jar (approximately 3 to 7 days).

4. Give the sprouts a final rinse; then remove and dry them. Eat within a few days.

In warmer climates,
sow 'Easter Egg' radishes in late winter
for harvest around Easter.
The multicolored mix produces
little oval radishes in red, white, pink, and
purple, like dyed Easter eggs.

Plant a few radish seeds
along with carrot seeds.
The radishes will
break through the soil first
and help carrots do the same.

The "baby" carrots available
in groceries are actually
regular-sized carrots cut and
smoothed down by a lathe.
Grow your own baby-sized carrots by
choosing small varieties,
such as 'Thumbelina'.

Spinach grows just like lettuce but is hardier in cold weather. It bolts as soon as weather heats up and days get longer. Choose from Savoy types, which have crinkled leaves, or flat-leaved varieties.

No gardener plants
only one thing. Yes, industrial
agriculture does that,
but no gardener would
think of such nonsense.
Gardeners balance high plants
with low plants, top growers
with bottom growers, vegetables
with flowers. The gardener learns
about crowding plants, about
earthworms, soil tilth, and a host
of comparisons and contrasts
that create a vibrant place.

Joel Salatin, *Folks, This Ain't Normal*

Just as in a natural ecosystem or a
human society, diversity will make a garden
more stable and therefore sustainable.
Grow a variety of plants in the same bed,
rather than planting a bed with all one crop.
Monoculture attracts pests,
while diversity confuses them.

PEPPERS and other summer veggies need heat to get started indoors. A heat mat is worth the cost, but you can also look for warm spots in your house, possibly the top of your fridge or near an oven or heat vent.

Use a soilless seed-starting mix instead of garden or potting soil to start seeds indoors. Seed-starting mix generally contains peat moss or coir along with vermiculite or perlite and has a fine, even texture that's good for germination and early plant growth.

Open-pollinated varieties are
pollinated naturally, by insects, wind,
or other factors. These varieties will produce a
new generation similar to the previous one.

Heirlooms are a subset of
open-pollinated varieties well known
for their flavors and stories.
Each heirloom variety can be traced back
through families and written or
oral history to the first gardeners who
grew it and passed its seed along.

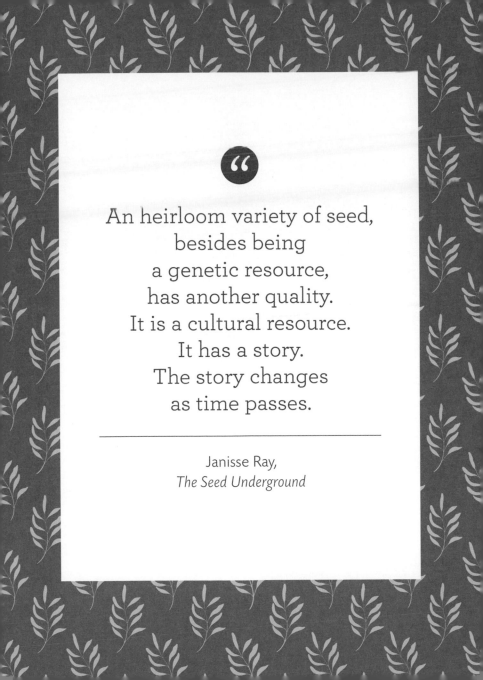

> **"**
>
> An heirloom variety of seed,
> besides being
> a genetic resource,
> has another quality.
> It is a cultural resource.
> It has a story.
> The story changes
> as time passes.

Janisse Ray,
The Seed Underground

HYBRID SEEDS are produced by controlled methods using pollen from different varieties or species, with the aim of getting characteristics of both. Be aware that when you grow hybrids, you can't save the seeds for next year and expect similar results. The offspring may be weaker and won't have the same characteristics as the plant from which you harvested the seed.

There are thousands of tomato varieties,
both open pollinated (including heirlooms)
and hybrid. Look for those adapted
to your region's specific conditions,
with descriptions like "cool climate,"
"heat tolerant," "early maturing,"
and "disease resistant."

"Hardening off" means acclimating seedlings from a regulated indoor environment to an unpredictable outdoor one. It's preschool for plants, where they learn to deal with shifting sunlight, temperatures, and moisture levels. Before transplanting them, harden off your seedlings by placing them in a cold frame or shady spot outside for a few hours at a time over a few days.

Like a mini greenhouse on the ground, **a cold frame**
can be used to grow crops during winter and to
transition seedlings from indoors to outdoors.
DIY cold frames can be made from wood and old windows,
or even with straw-bale walls and a window for a roof.

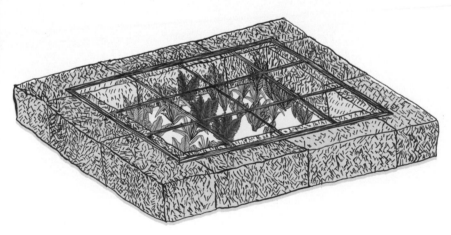

Walking on soil compacts it,

limiting movement of
air and water and making it
unfriendly for roots.
When planning your garden,
factor in walking space
but keep it minimal.

Avoid working in sopping-wet soil: disturbing it too much can also cause soil compaction. Wait for the soil to dry out a little before digging and planting.

I have become so confident of having a constant supply of food that often when I decide to grow things I can eat they have to transcend the ordinary: they must have a different color than the usual; they must have a different shape; they must come from far away; they must be the favorite food of the people in the countryside of France or Italy, or in the mountains of Peru.

Jamaica Kincaid, *My Garden (Book)*

◇◇

Order seed potatoes from certified growers rather than trying to grow from supermarket potatoes, which can spread disease and might be treated with chemicals (to prevent sprouting). Seed catalogs are full of interesting varieties. Growing potato varieties that are hard to find or expensive to buy is well worth it.

◇◇

Handling a seedling by the stem
can lead to harmful breaks or bruises.
Instead, to transplant, scoop up a little
soil under the seedling to support it
from the roots. If you must, you can
lightly touch the leaves.

TRUE LEAVES

COTYLEDONS

Most seedlings have two types of leaves: seed leaves, or *cotyledons*, which appear first, and true leaves, which appear second and look like mini versions of a plant's mature leaves. After true leaves appear, you can consider carefully fertilizing, thinning, or repotting the seedlings.

"Full sun" means at least six hours per day.
Some vegetable plants grown for fruit, like tomatoes and
eggplant, prefer more, while others grown for leaves,
such as lettuce, survive with a little less.

Perhaps more than any other vegetable,
eggplant needs hot summer weather to grow well.
If you live in a northern climate with a shorter
growing season, plan to grow eggplant
in large containers, where the smaller amount
of soil will heat up faster.

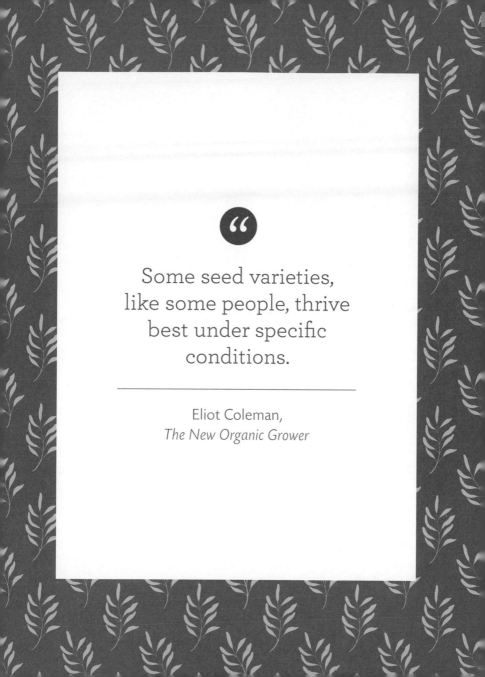

> **"**
>
> Some seed varieties, like some people, thrive best under specific conditions.

Eliot Coleman,
The New Organic Grower

Broccoli grows best between 65°F and 80°F. An extended cold snap below 40°F may cause it to bloom too early, and a heat wave can trigger the same issue.

Start cauliflower indoors and set out transplants after the last frost date in spring so the plant will mature before summer. This helps dodge two things cauliflower hates: hard frost and hot weather.

Try regrowing celery, whether homegrown or store-bought, from the base of the stalk, a part most people toss. Place the base in a shallow bowl of water indoors on a sunny windowsill. Refresh the water daily. Watch for signs of regrowth from the center. Transplant outside in spring when temperatures are staying above 40°F at night and 55°F during the day.

◇◇◇◇◇◇◇◇◇◇◇◇◇◇◇◇◇◇◇◇◇◇◇◇◇◇◇◇◇◇◇◇◇◇◇◇◇◇◇

Each beet "seed" is actually a fruit
that contains up to six seeds.
They germinate better if soaked
in water an hour or so before planting,
either in summer for fall harvest
or early spring for summer harvest.

◇◇◇◇◇◇◇◇◇◇◇◇◇◇◇◇◇◇◇◇◇◇◇◇◇◇◇◇◇◇◇◇◇◇◇◇◇◇◇

When beet greens
are about an inch tall,
thin them so plants are
4 inches apart. Mound
soil around each plant,
giving more coverage
for roots to grow.

Melons, including watermelon, cantaloupe, and honeydew, need two to three months of hot weather, making them harder to grow in northern climates. Give them a head start indoors on a heat mat, and use black plastic to heat the soil around them after transplanting.

ROW COVER, a lightweight,
partially transparent fabric,
can be a plant saver:
use it to shield plants during
frost, hold in warmth and
moisture during a cold snap, and
protect young plants from pests.

'Moon and Stars' is a
particularly interesting
Amish heirloom watermelon
variety with spots
on the rind instead of stripes:
one large yellow "moon"
spot and several little
yellow "stars."

SEED LIBRARIES, often housed in public libraries or community centers, act as local seed banks. Gardeners can check out seeds and grow them for a season with the promise of saving and returning the seeds to the library at season's end.

Gently touching and even
shaking your plants, particularly those
grown indoors, can help them
grow better. It encourages plants to respond
as though in their natural habitat
(for example, growing thicker, shorter stems
in the face of potentially damaging wind).

> "
>
> No matter how
> the harvest will turn out,
> whether or not there
> will be enough food to eat,
> in simply sowing seed
> and caring tenderly for
> plants under nature's guidance
> there is joy.

Masanobu Fukuoka,
The One-Straw Revolution

SPRING
PLANTING &
TENDING

◇◇◇◇◇◇◇◇◇◇◇◇◇◇◇◇

Like stretching for the race ahead, spring's slower, simpler pleasures are an enjoyable way to gear up for summer. This season is all about rediscovering freshness and revitalizing my body, the earth, and my taste buds. For me, nothing rivals tangy, spicy arugula picked and eaten right there in the garden . . . unless it's the first red radish plucked straight from the soil.

Peas are one of the first things
you can plant outside in early spring.
Soak pea seeds for about 24 hours
before planting to soften the hard seed
exterior and speed up germination.

Sugar snap peas are a
cross between garden (shelling) peas and
snow peas, offering the best of both worlds:
crunchy, edible pods, and sweet, succulent peas.
Sugar snap seeds have only been
on the market since the 1970s.

The garden is a lot
like a puppy: it needs care
and attention every day.
And like a puppy,
it pays you back with
endless rewards,
the kiss of bloom on fruit,
the sweet fullness
of a fresh pea.

Deborah Madison,
Vegetable Literacy

Even dwarf varieties of peas
grow best with some
support from a trellis.
Chicken wire is a good option,
or make use of your tomato
cages out of season and use
them for peas in spring.

Try planting **carrots** at the base of your pea trellis. Getting along "like peas and carrots" isn't just a cliché. The plants make good garden companions and can be harvested together.

Remove blossoms from
pepper transplants before setting
them out in the garden and
for a couple of weeks after planting.
This gives the plant an opportunity
to put energy into roots and
leaves before pumping out peppers.

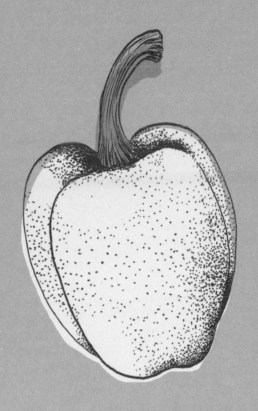

Keep in mind that despite their affinity for heat, **peppers** can suffer from sunscald (basically a sunburn) if leaf cover isn't sufficient. Growing peppers near taller, leafier plants, like tomatoes, can help.

Tomato varieties are generally classified in one of two ways:

Indeterminate: The plant will grow indefinitely until killed by frost.

Determinate: The plant will grow to a certain height and stop. Choose determinate tomato varieties (sometimes called "bush" or "compact" tomatoes) for growing in containers.

An early tomato variety typically matures in less than 60 days, as opposed to regular varieties that can take 75 to 100 days. Early tomatoes are best for gardeners in cool climates with a short growing season.

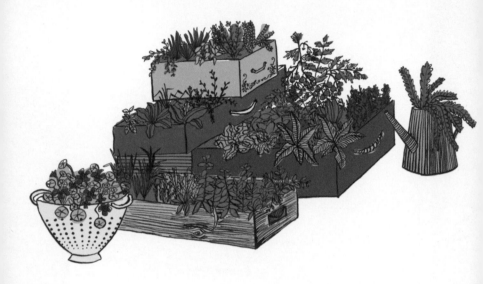

The first rule of thumb for container gardening? Containers
must have drainage holes. Beyond that, nearly anything can
make a great container, not just flowerpots but barrels, buckets,
and bins, even old toolboxes or furniture. Just add drainage holes
and you're in business. Containers are a chance to be creative!

Save money on potting soil
and reduce weight in a
large container by using filler
material at the bottom, such as
plastic bottles or leftover
plant containers. Cover with
landscape fabric and then soil.
This method also helps with
drainage and airflow to provide
good habitat for growing roots.
Just make sure drainage holes
aren't impeded and the plant
still has the right amount
of soil depth.

MULCH SHADES SOIL to reduce water
evaporation and limit weed growth,
protects plants from soilborne diseases
that can be transferred when water splashes
onto leaves, prevents soil erosion, and
decomposes to add nutrients to the soil.

Straw and hay

aren't the same thing.
For mulch, use straw —
hay contains seeds that will
sprout in your garden.

After compost itself, mulches in general are the subject most actively boring to the organic gardener's friends.

Eleanor Perényi,
Green Thoughts

◇◇

Newspaper makes a good first-layer mulch.
Conventional wisdom used to be to use
only pages with soy-based black inks to avoid
the petroleum-derived colored inks.
These days, however, most newspaper inks
of all shades are made from soy.
If you're concerned, check to be sure.

◇◇

Cabbage-family plants (a.k.a. "brassicas") include cabbage, kale, cauliflower, kohlrabi, broccoli, rutabaga, and Brussels sprouts. All prefer cool weather and can be planted in early spring or late summer for fall growing.

Cabbage's days

to maturity vary widely among varieties, from as few as 50 days to as many as 125. Varieties called "late" take longer to mature but are great for the fall season and for storage and preserving, while those labeled "early" are best for spring and will be ready sooner for eating fresh.

◇◇◇◇◇◇◇◇◇◇◇◇◇◇◇◇◇◇◇◇◇◇◇◇◇◇◇◇◇◇◇◇◇◇◇◇◇◇

Lettuce varieties come in
two main types: heading and leaf.
HEADING LETTUCES need more space
and are harvested at once, as a single head.
LEAF LETTUCES are good for containers
and small spaces, making them perfect for
growing on patios or balconies and in
window boxes, even those without full sun.

◇◇◇◇◇◇◇◇◇◇◇◇◇◇◇◇◇◇◇◇◇◇◇◇◇◇◇◇◇◇◇◇◇◇◇◇◇◇

Plant lettuce among cool-season crops,
like carrots, beets, cabbage, Brussels sprouts, and other
cabbage-family plants, where the lettuce will
keep the soil shaded, acting as a living mulch that
reduces weed growth and maintains soil moisture.

Sow lettuce seeds on top of the soil and
cover only lightly with soil or seed-starting mix –
they need sunlight to germinate.

Nestle thyme, mint, rosemary, dill, and sage among your cabbage-family crops — the strong scents of these particular herbs can repel the cabbage moths that become hungry cabbage worms.

Remember that mint grows "like a weed," and many gardeners consider it invasive. Give it a spot of its own or plant it in a pot, where it won't spread. If you want to grow mint alongside other plants to repel insect pests, you can partially bury the pot in your in-ground or raised-bed garden.

Mix green and red lettuces with pansies for easy,
cool-season color.

Leaf lettuces, spinach, chard, and mustard
can be grown with the "cut-and-come-again" method.
Cut all leaves to an inch above the soil and
allow them to grow back.

Meal planning is simply more exciting and less bewildering when you wait for fruits and vegetables to come into season, eat them steadily when they arrive, and say a reluctant goodbye for another year when their season has passed.

Joan Dye Gussow,
This Organic Life: Confessions of a Suburban Homesteader

**DON'T LIMIT YOUR
PICKLING TO CUCUMBERS.**
Spring crops, like carrots, beets, and radishes,
also make great pickled veggies. Pair these
earthy root vegetables with similarly grounding
spices, such as cinnamon, clove, and ginger.

RADISHES MAY LOSE THEIR FIRMNESS AFTER YOU BRING THEM INSIDE. Soak them in ice water for a half hour or so (before or after slicing) and they'll perk up.

. . . .

BUTTER SOFTENS THE PIQUANCY OF RADISHES TO PERFECTION. Fresh, raw radishes with butter and salt make a simple, classic combo, but also try sautéing or roasting the radishes with butter, finishing with coarse sea salt.

Discovering the varieties
of beans that were grown
by gardening enthusiasts was
like the first time I ate
a 'Cherokee Purple' heirloom
tomato. The skies cleared,
the heavens opened up,
and I was eating well.
Heirloom beans have been an
obsession ever since.

Steve Sando,
*The Rancho Gordo Heirloom
Bean Grower's Guide*

Black-eyed peas (known as southern peas in the South)
are actually beans, members of the cowpea family
of legumes. Cowpeas originated in West Africa and also
include crowder peas, pink-eyed peas, and asparagus
(or yard-long) beans.

For small spaces, try "bush" varieties of beans,
which don't need to be staked or trellised. You can even
grow some bush bean varieties in containers.

June-bearing strawberry varieties

ripen as one large crop
in late spring to early summer,
making them best for preserving.
Ever-bearing varieties ripen
in early summer and also in
late summer and early fall,
but never a lot at one time,
making them better for picking
and eating fresh.

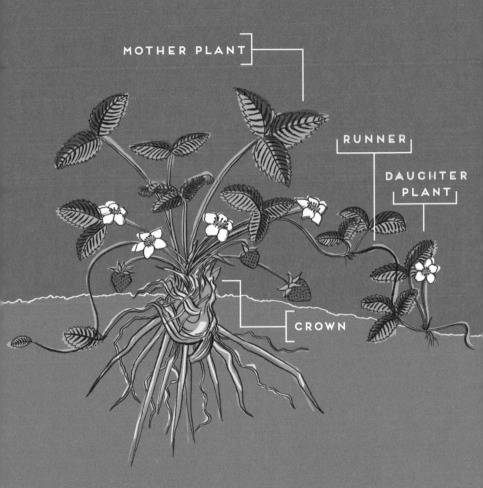

MOTHER PLANT

RUNNER

DAUGHTER PLANT

CROWN

The thick center of a strawberry plant, called the "crown," grows roots from its base and new leaves and flowers from its top. Be careful not to bury the crown when planting. It will send out runners that will root and form new plants, called "daughter" plants. To keep the "mother" plant healthy and producing well, clip back all or some of these runners.

ASPARAGUS CAN PRODUCE

in the same spot for up to 20 years, so choose carefully when planning and planting, and give it a dedicated spot without competition. In the early years, the harvest season may be only a few weeks, but established plants will produce longer, up to 8 weeks.

Most gardeners plant asparagus from
crowns, typically one-year-old plants.
This is easier than starting from seed
and gives you a leg up toward harvesting,
since asparagus spears shouldn't be harvested
until the plants are about three years old.

THE DISTINCTIVE FLAVOR OF ASPARAGUS
is identified by food scientists as a fifth taste,
umami, beyond the four long-recognized ones:
sweet, sour, salty, and bitter. Asparagus
and its umami flavor are best fresh
from the garden. If you must wait, store the
cut spears standing up in a container filled
with a few inches of water.

Satisfaction was seeing the tips of the asparagus poke through the earth, coming all the way up, wonderfully whole, real, and without blemish, just the way they should be really, from the trenches into which I placed their roots.

Jamaica Kincaid, *My Garden (Book)*

◇◇◇

A PH TEST (available at garden centers) measures whether soil is acidic (below 7.0), alkaline (above 7.0), or neutral (7.0). The recommended pH for general vegetable gardening is about 6.5. Organic material and agricultural sulfur will lower pH, while lime and wood ash will raise it.

◇◇◇

Blueberries

need much more
acidic soil (pH 5.5 or lower)
than most garden vegetables,
so it's best to grow
blueberries in their own
dedicated patch.

A fertile soil,
like an educated mind,
is a cumulative process,
and with care it is capable
of continuous improvement.

Eliot Coleman,
The New Organic Grower

Good compost has the right balance of "brown" and "green" materials, about two-thirds brown and one-third green. Slower-decomposing browns include straw, leaves, and brown paper. Greens, which break down faster, include grass clippings and kitchen scraps. The most common mistake backyard composters make is to tip the ratio in their compost more "green" than "brown." If your compost feels soppy or smells funky, try adding more brown materials, such as straw, dried leaves, or shredded newspaper.

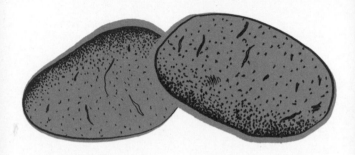

◇◇

After cutting seed potatoes
into pieces with a couple of eyes each,
let the pieces dry out on the cut sides
for a few days before planting them —
this helps retain moisture and prevent rot.

◇◇

In small spaces, grow potatoes in containers or in flexible, permeable bags. When it's time to harvest, dump the bag out and collect your potatoes. Some even have a flap for checking on potatoes growing under the soil or harvesting a few early (or new) potatoes without disturbing the whole crop.

GROW ONIONS from seed
(which takes longest), from transplants
(which are most susceptible to diseases),
or from sets, immature bulbs grown the
previous year (which are quickest and
easiest but prone to bolting).

Scallions (or "green" or "spring" onions) are just immature onions. Double up your spacing for onions, then harvest every other one as a scallion during spring. Leave those left to reach full size.

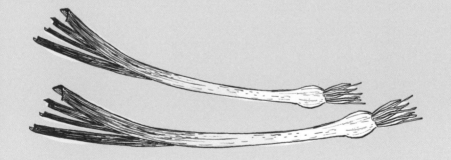

PLANT ONIONS among your other crops for natural pest control. Onion-family plants (including garlic) have a characteristic smell that deters many garden pests, such as aphids, ants, and flea beetles.

The chemical compounds that make
you cry when **CHOPPING ONIONS** are also
what help onions store for so long.
(Sweet onions taste milder because they
have less of these compounds,
but this, along with higher water content,
means they won't store well.)
To reduce tears when chopping onions,
cut the root end, where the compounds
are concentrated, last.
Chilling before chopping also helps.

Plant sweet potatoes from slips,
cuttings grown from a mature sweet potato.
You can order these from catalogs or online,
or buy transplants that have been
grown using slips.

SWEET POTATOES aren't related
to potatoes or yams but are members
of the morning-glory family, and
unlike regular potato leaves, which
are poisonous, sweet potato leaves
are totally edible. They're also
loaded with vitamins and are popular
in Asian and African cuisine. To eat,
remove the leaves from the stems
and use them as you would spinach.
For a simple Asian-inspired side,
try sautéing them with
sesame oil and ginger.

"Pie" pumpkin varieties are small and dense,
with more pulp per inch for making pie purée.
The plants are also more compact than regular varieties,
and they mature more quickly, making them
an all-around good garden pick.

When planting squash, pumpkins, or melons
from seed, create a mound of soil a few inches high
and plant a few seeds in each mound.
This helps keep soil warm and well drained.

However blessed you may be
with imagination, and
whatever may have been your
many years of experience,
it seems impossible,
when you put in hills of
squash in spring, for you to be
able to visualize how far
they will probably
wander before frost.

Ruth Stout, *Gardening Without Work*

Even if pea pods are past their prime,
remove them from the plant and compost them.
Leaving overmature pods on the plant signals the
plant to stop producing more peas.

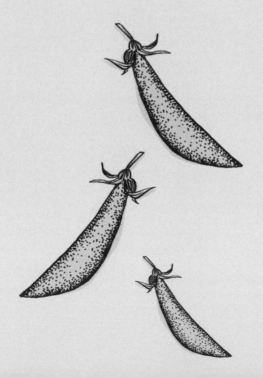

PEA-SHOOT SALAD

Make a pea-shoot salad using the tender, edible vines, leaves, and flowers.

1. Harvest the growing tips of pea plants you're also growing for pods, or harvest some solely for their greens as you thin them.

2. Toss 5 to 6 cups of pea shoots with a little olive oil and lemon juice.

3. Top with shaved Parmesan and freshly ground black pepper.

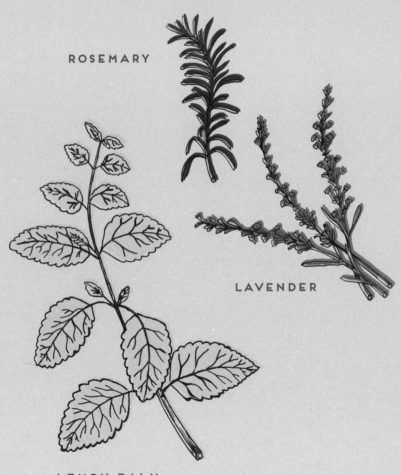

ROSEMARY

LAVENDER

LEMON BALM

Many favorite culinary herbs are
members of the mint family, including peppermint,
spearmint, bee balm, sage, lavender, basil, oregano,
thyme, lemon balm, and rosemary.
You can easily identify mint-family plants
by their square stems.

Mints play an important role in gardens
by attracting pollinators, including honeybees,
with their fragrant leaves and flowers.
The botanical name for lemon balm,
Melissa, even means honeybee in Greek.

Things want to grow,
I'd discovered;
you just need
to learn how to stop
getting in the way.

———————————————————

Jeanne Nolan,
From the Ground Up

Plant rosemary, lavender, sage, tarragon, oregano, thyme, and most other herbs in a pot or somewhere in the garden where they will get good drainage, then leave them alone. These plants typically don't need fertilizer or much water.

CHIVES deter pest insects
and grow well in pots. Trim them often,
and they'll grow back quickly
for multiple harvests in a season.
But also allow some
to go to seed so you can enjoy
the pretty purple blossoms,
which attract pollinators and make
a perfect edible garnish.
Use them for a pop of color
and flavor on luncheon favorites
like cucumber sandwiches
and potato salad.

DILL serves as host plant for the beautiful swallowtail butterfly (as does parsley). You may spot the black-, yellow-, and green-striped caterpillars along the plant's stem. They're worth the sacrifice of a little dill, which grows easily and abundantly in summer, attracting many other beneficial insects and pollinators.

Insects are considered "beneficial" in the garden if they help with pollination, prey on garden pests, or decompose wastes to create soil and compost. Honeybees, ladybugs, green lacewings, and ground beetles are some familiar beneficials.

Attract beneficial insects with a diversity of flowers, creating a year-round habitat called an insectary. Include self-sowing herbs (like cilantro, chamomile, and dill) with annual and perennial flowers (like sunflowers, cosmos, zinnia, yarrow, black-eyed Susan, coneflower, coreopsis, and calendula). In larger spaces, plant a border garden or bed, but in smaller spaces, even a container insectary will make a difference.

When soil has warmed up to about 60°F,
heat-loving tomato transplants are ready
for the outdoors. Plant them deep in the soil,
burying all but about 4 inches of plant.
The buried stems will become roots.

Place tomato supports, like stakes and cages,
when you plant to avoid disturbing
precious roots later on. Even smaller
determinate plants benefit from support,
and for indeterminate plants, it's a necessity.

Most of the good gardeners
I've met seem to possess
a faculty, akin to empathy,
that allows them to sense
what their plants might need
at any time.

Michael Pollan,
Second Nature: A Gardener's Education

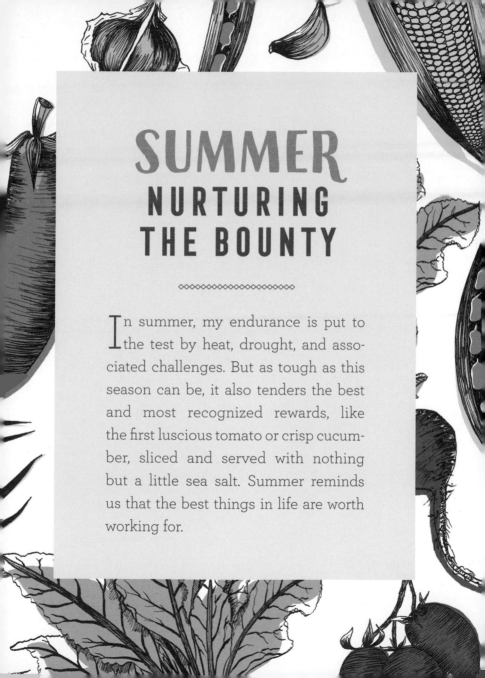

SUMMER
NURTURING
THE BOUNTY

◇◇◇◇◇◇◇◇◇◇◇◇◇◇◇◇◇◇

In summer, my endurance is put to the test by heat, drought, and associated challenges. But as tough as this season can be, it also tenders the best and most recognized rewards, like the first luscious tomato or crisp cucumber, sliced and served with nothing but a little sea salt. Summer reminds us that the best things in life are worth working for.

Water plants early in the morning to
reduce evaporation from heat. It can also be
a nice, meditative way to start your day —
think of it as a mindfulness practice.

Similarly, instead of thinking of
weeding as a chore, think of weeds as
metaphors for anything unwanted or
unneeded, such as negative thoughts,
relationships, or habits. Removing
literal weeds may help you remove
figurative ones as well.

> Something happens to me when I garden. I am fully, reliably, blissfully present to who I am and where I am in that moment.

Janisse Ray,
The Seed Underground

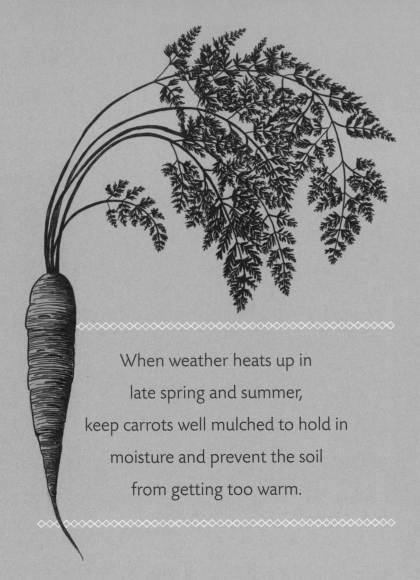

When weather heats up in
late spring and summer,
keep carrots well mulched to hold in
moisture and prevent the soil
from getting too warm.

For root crops,

too much nitrogen results in lush green tops but meager roots that, in the case of carrots and parsnips, can be forked or twisty instead of long and straight. Be careful not to overfeed them or grow in too-rich soil.

CARROT-TOP PESTO

Don't toss carrot tops! These overlooked greens are completely edible and taste a bit like their cousin, parsley. Preserve raw carrot greens by making carrot-top pesto.

1. Pulse together 1½ cups coarsely chopped carrot greens, ¼ cup roasted nuts (such as pecans or cashews), 1 clove garlic, and ½ cup olive oil.

2. Add ¼ cup grated Parmesan.

3. Adjust the ingredients to get a consistency you like.

WAIT TO PULL UP CARROTS until after the roots begin to push up out of the soil. To keep the exposed tops from turning green, you can hill up a little soil around them until harvest.

The reason cauliflower heads stay so white is a labor-intensive practice called blanching — the leaves are manually folded and secured over the head to block sunlight. If you're not up for doing this by hand, choose self-blanching varieties with leaves that curl around the head naturally, or go for purple, green, or orange varieties that don't require blanching and look fun on the plate.

Cut broccoli heads with a sharp knife
at a slight angle to prevent moisture from pooling up
and making the plant susceptible to fungal issues.

After you harvest the main head of broccoli,
leave the plant to produce harvestable side shoots
with smaller heads.

Beans and peas secure much of their own nitrogen requirements through bacteria called rhizobia that live in their roots. When the plants die, any nitrogen stored (or fixed) in the roots is released back into the soil. This is one reason peas and beans are often building blocks of a succession-planting plan — they enrich the soil for plants coming after, including nitrogen lovers, like tomatoes, squash, and cucumbers.

As I think back,
it seems clear that the
first serious sign of our move
toward vegetal self-reliance
was when we stopped
planting everything
in the spring.

Joan Dye Gussow,
*This Organic Life: Confessions of a
Suburban Homesteader*

Succession planting is the practice of
staggering planting times to extend the season.
For example, peas have a short life,
so if you plant some every few weeks you can
draw out the harvest window. This works
for lettuces and greens, like arugula, too.
The term can also mean replacing one crop
with another as the seasons change,
such as removing spring peas to plant
heat-loving peppers.

Coffee grounds

are especially good for your compost pile or for working directly into garden soil. Alongside organic fertilizer, they'll contribute nitrogen and improve soil consistency.

Nitrogen promotes green leaves.
If plant leaves are yellow, it may be a lack of
nitrogen in the soil. Add compost, blood meal
(a by-product of the meat industry), or fish emulsion
(a by-product of the fishing industry).

Phosphorus also keeps your leaves green.
A purple tint to leaves, particularly leaf veins,
may mean your soil needs more of it.
Amend with rock phosphate or organic
bonemeal before the next planting.

LETTUCE grows best in cool weather
but can grow through summer if
given some shade. Plant it at the base
of taller summer crops, like tomatoes,
or in the shadow of a cucumber
or bean trellis.

ARUGULA (sometimes called "rocket")
grows fast. Pick leaves when young and tender,
as older leaves can be tougher and taste bitter.
As the plant flowers and stops producing leaves,
you can still snip and use the edible blooms,
which retain some of the characteristic
spicy arugula flavor.

Pick greens,

such as kale, collards, mustard, and Swiss chard, from the bottom of the plant up and from the outside in. Keep the top and center leaves in place, and the plant will continue to grow.

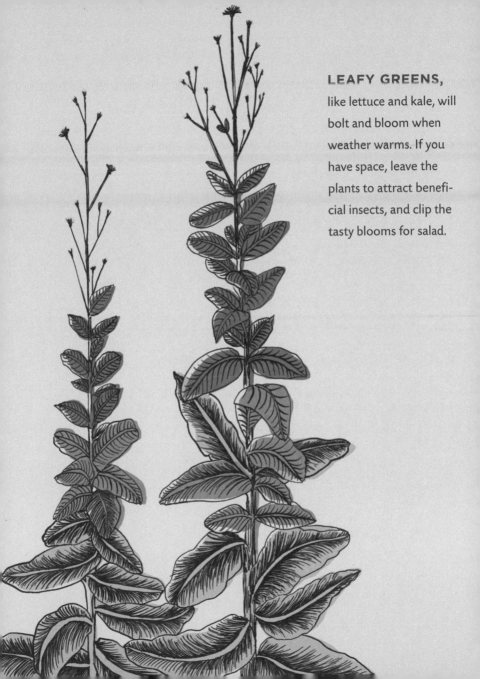

LEAFY GREENS, like lettuce and kale, will bolt and bloom when weather warms. If you have space, leave the plants to attract beneficial insects, and clip the tasty blooms for salad.

Water is taken up by roots and
drawn into a plant's stems and leaves.
Watering leaves isn't necessary and can actually
make plants more susceptible to disease,
so water at the base of the plant to get moisture
where it's needed most: the roots.

Water the entire garden bed,
not just the area directly around the plant.
This will encourage roots to extend
far deeper and wider.

If a plant is stressed from
too little or too much water or
not enough nutrients from the soil,
it will be more susceptible to pests.
The first line of defense against
pests is to grow plants in the
best possible conditions.

"Burpless" cucumber varieties are
bred to reduce the amount of cucurbitacin,
a bitter-tasting natural chemical
that may cause burping. These varieties
are generally sweeter and thinner skinned
than regular cucumbers but are
otherwise grown in the same manner.

PICKLING CUCUMBER VARIETIES

are typically shorter and have rougher skin
than varieties for eating fresh.

GROW DILL alongside pickling cucumbers in
anticipation of making pickles. Sow the herbs in
succession, seeding every few weeks, to ensure
a constant supply well timed with your
cuke harvest. When blooming, the dill will also
attract pollinators to the cucumber plants.

REFRIGERATOR PICKLES

Making pickles doesn't always mean a lot of time, supplies, or cleanup. Get some pickling practice with this easy refrigerator recipe, no canning required, and then adapt it for other veggies.

1. Combine 1 cup vinegar, ¼ cup water, ¼ cup sugar, and 1 teaspoon salt to make a brine.

2. Heat until the sugar dissolves.

3. Pack 2 cups sliced cucumbers into a jar, and add a few garlic cloves and some fresh dill leaves and flowers.

4. Pour the hot brine over the cucumbers so that they are completely covered with liquid. Screw on the lid.

5. Keep in the fridge for a month.

Insecticides and fungicides, whether organic or not, should be sprayed sparingly and purposefully, as they could affect beneficial insects as well as harmful ones. Typically, the best time to spray is early in the morning or late in the evening when plants are shaded and will stay wet longer.

Neem oil is an organic insecticide and fungicide made from the neem tree of tropical Africa and Asia. It's known to be safe for beneficial insects, including honeybees, as well as earthworms, and is a good solution to a range of common problems, from aphids and mites to powdery mildew.

GARLIC REPELLENT

Garlic repels many harmful bugs, including aphids, ants, and slugs, so it can make a useful insect repellent.

1. Steep a chopped garlic bulb in a quart of water to make a tea. You can also add onion and cayenne.

2. Mix the tea with a tablespoon of dish soap in a spray bottle.

3. Spray on undersides of plant leaves. Store extra in the refrigerator.

GROW CORN IN BLOCKS rather than rows to promote complete pollination by wind and ensure fully formed ears. For example, in a small garden, grow 16 plants 1 foot apart in a 4 x 4-foot bed.

CORN IS WIND POLLINATED IN FIELDS, but you can hand-pollinate small amounts of corn by tapping the pollen-laden tassels over the silks at the point where they emerge from the ears.

I have never felt that a vegetable grown in an open field tastes as good as one grown in a small garden. Our garden, when I was a child, was a pampered piece of soil outside the kitchen window, nurtured with compost, ashes from the wood stove, and manure from the barnyard.

Edna Lewis, *In Pursuit of Flavor*

PLANTS IN THE GOURD FAMILY

(or cucurbits, including squash, cucumbers, melons, and pumpkins) produce both male and female flowers. Pollen is transferred (typically by bees) from the male flower to the female flower, where fruit develops. Female flowers are larger than males and have a small developing fruit between the bloom and stem.

SQUASH VINE BORERS, a species of sesiid moth, overwinter in soil and then tunnel into squash stems and eat their way through, leaving sawdust-like frass (or waste) behind. Wrapping lower stems with a little aluminum foil may slow borers, but there's really no way to stop them. If they're a problem (particularly in warmer regions like the South), look for borer-resistant varieties, or plant summer squash in large containers, where they will look great and thrive.

The blossoms of all squash varieties are edible, but don't pick them all or you won't have any fruit. Male flowers arrive first — pick a few of these and leave a few to pollinate the female flowers that arrive later.

You'll know garlic is ready for harvest
when some of the leaves start
to turn from green to yellow. Loosen soil around
the bulbs, if needed, and pull up the
entire plant. You don't need to wait until
the tops turn brown and flop over
like onions, garlic's cousin.

MAKE YOUR OWN GARLIC POWDER

by drying sliced garlic cloves in a food
dehydrator and then grinding them
with a coffee grinder.

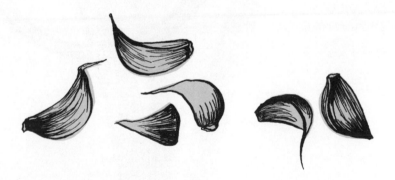

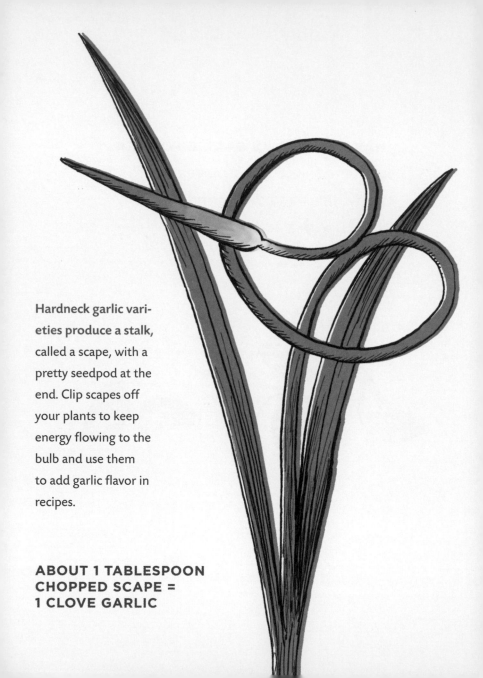

Hardneck garlic varieties produce a stalk, called a scape, with a pretty seedpod at the end. Clip scapes off your plants to keep energy flowing to the bulb and use them to add garlic flavor in recipes.

ABOUT 1 TABLESPOON CHOPPED SCAPE = 1 CLOVE GARLIC

ROASTED GARLIC

Roasting whole garlic softens both the flavor and the texture, making it easier to use the cloves in a variety of dishes or to enjoy them alone or simply spread on toasted bread.

1. Remove much of the bulb's papery outer skin.

2. Cut the top ¼ inch or so off the cloves so each is revealed inside its skin.

3. Place the bulb on foil in a skillet or muffin tin, drizzle with olive oil, close the foil around it, and bake at 400°F for 40 minutes.

4. Cool and unwrap. Remove caramelized cloves to spread on bread, mash into potatoes, mix in salad dressing, or eat on their own.

When potato plants are about
8 inches tall, mound or "hill" soil
around the stem, covering two thirds
of the plant. Keep hilling as the plant
grows, so the stem will produce more
potatoes. Only the top 6 inches or so
should remain uncovered.

How worms love
these hilled-up crops
to frolic in, leaving
behind their own
goodness as another
thank-you note.

Margaret Roach,
And I Shall Have Some Peace There

Potato blossoms
indicate the skin color
of the potatoes:
tan potatoes have white
flowers, blue have purple,
and red have pink.

GREEN LACEWINGS

eat aphids, spider mites, caterpillar eggs, and many other garden pests. Their beautiful bright green color resembles so many plants' leaves that you may miss them, but they're worth observing. They may take care of an aphid problem for you.

> **"**
>
> Every harmful insect
> has a mortal enemy.
> Cultivate that enemy
> and he will do
> your work for you.

Eleanor Perényi,
Green Thoughts

MANY PARASITIC WASPS are pollinators as well as predators of garden pests like aphids,tomato hornworms, cabbage worms, and cutworms. And, thankfully, they don't sting humans.

There are more than 450 species of ladybugs in North America, some native and some introduced. Most are considered benign or beneficial in the garden, though a recently introduced Asian lady beetle species (identified by the white "M" mark behind its head) will move inside homes in winter and become a nuisance.

Okra's beautiful white bloom with a deep red center
may look familiar — it's a member of the mallow family,
closely related to hibiscus and cotton. Like its cousins,
it thrives in hot climates.

In many parts of the world, okra is referred to as *gumbo*,
a word derived from West African languages.
In the United States, gumbo also refers to a dish
that sometimes includes okra.

CUT OKRA PODS
when they're 2 to 3 inches
long, though some varieties
will stay tender longer.
Pods that are too long will
be fibrous and tough. Pick
daily when ripening —
okra has a tendency to get
away from you.

Snipping the flower buds off herbs,
such as basil and oregano, promotes fuller plants
with more leaves for harvest, but
it means you miss out on the edible flowers,
which can attract beneficial insects.
If you have space, maintain some herbs for their
leaves while letting others fully bloom.

CILANTRO grows best in cool weather
and bolts (or blooms) in warm weather,
when you can harvest the seeds
as they begin to turn brown.
Grind the seeds into fragrant
coriander spice using a
coffee grinder or mortar and pestle.

Plant basil near tomatoes —
not only are they a
great combo in the kitchen,
basil's smell confuses
some tomato-loving insect pests.

CLASSIC BASIL PESTO

Basil doesn't do well in the refrigerator, developing black spots of fungus quickly. The best way to preserve basil is by making pesto, then freezing it in small bags or ice cube trays so you can thaw out small servings one at a time. Adapt this classic basil pesto recipe by changing up the greens and nuts, or omitting cheese.

1. Place ½ cup olive oil, ½ cup Parmesan cheese, 2 cups fresh basil leaves, 3 tablespoons pine nuts, and 2 to 3 garlic cloves in a food processor or blender, and process into a paste.

2. Add salt and pepper if desired.

3. Use a tablespoon or two fresh as a pasta sauce, to top grilled fish or chicken, or as an appetizer spread. Store the remainder in an airtight container in the refrigerator or in the freezer as noted above.

Harvest garlic and onions when the soil is dry. Don't wash the dirt off the bulbs. Either cure them with the dirt on, or gently remove the dirt with your hands or a dry cloth.

GARLIC AND ONIONS need to be cured,
leaves attached, for two to three weeks,
in a well-ventilated spot where they won't get wet.
A covered porch, barn, or garage will do.
After the bulbs are cured, clip off the dry stems
to about an inch.

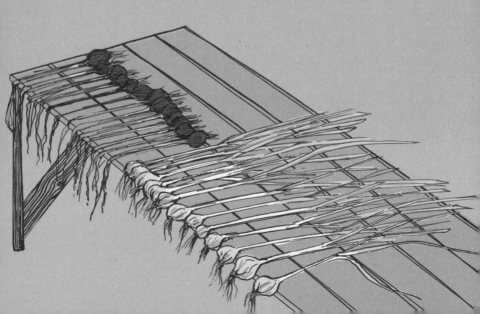

Garlic is divine.
Few food items can taste
so many distinct ways,
handled correctly.
Misuse of garlic is a crime . . .
Please, treat your
garlic with respect.

Anthony Bourdain,
Kitchen Confidential

Choose a few prime bulbs

from your garlic harvest to set aside

for the next season's planting.

Store garlic bulbs in a dry, cool, dark place,

preferably not in the refrigerator.

The blooms of some plants
need to be clipped back often to
keep them producing new flowers
all season. This includes many
flowers commonly grown alongside
vegetables, like French marigolds,
calendula, cosmos, borage, and
zinnia. Don't be shy about cutting
the flowers and bringing them inside
to enjoy — the more you snip, the
better for you and for the garden.

PLANT NASTURTIUM to fend off a variety of veggie pests, but don't forget to harvest it as an edible, too. The pretty lily-pad-like leaves taste similar to arugula, and the delicate flowers make a lovely garnish that's edible, too. Try making nasturtium-leaf pesto, replacing the basil with nasturtium, and decorate with a few spicy nasturtium blooms.

SUMMER

181

Damp weather is the enemy of the
tomato gardener because it fosters leaf spots and blights.
Do some local research and talk to neighbors
to find out what diseases are common in your area,
then grow resistant varieties.

A black spot on the bottom of a tomato is
likely blossom-end rot, a common condition caused
by calcium deficiency from moisture fluctuations.
Harvest the fruit and cut off the black portion
(the rest is perfectly fine to eat); then make sure
plants are well mulched and watered as consistently
as possible. End rot also occurs on peppers,
eggplant, and melons.

Tomato plants

need a steady supply of
nutrients, so plan on feeding
every few weeks with organic
fertilizer, such as fish emulsion.

Paste (or plum) tomatoes are firm, contain less water and fewer seeds than most varieties, and are often determinate (as in the case of the popular Roma), meaning all the fruits ripen around the same time. These traits make them ideal for making tomato sauce and salsa, fresh or canned.

"

Eating locally
in winter is easy.
But the time
to think about that
would be August.

Barbara Kingsolver,
Animal, Vegetable, Miracle

Cherry tomato

varieties produce clusters of small fruits that can be eaten whole. Their sweetness (because the sugars are more concentrated) makes them irresistible.

DEHYDRATED CHERRY TOMATOES

If you have a glut of cherry tomatoes, try dehydrating some. You can add salt or spices before drying, but it's not necessary — the sugars become concentrated, and you'll want to eat them as sweet snacks.

1. Halve each tomato and lay them cut-side up on dehydrator trays.

2. Dry for at least 8 hours at 125°F (or at least 4 hours on a parchment-lined baking sheet in a 200°F oven).

"

It's hard to
think sad thoughts
when you're
inhaling mint.

Diane Ackerman,
Cultivating Delight

Make your own peppermint or bee balm tea
by simply steeping the leaves in hot water.

◇◇

A MINT NATIVE TO NORTH AMERICA,
bee balm attracts bees, butterflies, and hummingbirds,
and the leaves make a lovely menthol-like tea.
It's also known as bergamot because it has an aroma similar
to that of bergamot orange, the distinctive ingredient in
Earl Grey tea.

SUMMER

189

CAPSAICIN is the compound in peppers
that makes them hot. Scoville heat units measure
how hot a pepper is based on the concentration of the
capsaicin in it, from bell pepper (0) to jalapeño (4,500),
cayenne (50,000), habanero (350,000), and beyond.

• •

The **HEAT** in hot peppers is mostly concentrated
in the ribs, not the seeds as many people think.
To tone down the heat, remove the white membrane
that attaches the seeds to the flesh of the pepper.
If a particularly hot pepper sets your mouth on fire,
reach for milk instead of water. Capsaicin is fat soluble
and better diminished by fats than water.

When the summer rains
poured it on again so hard that
I couldn't keep up with my own
backyard production of jalapeños,
guajillas, serranos, and *pasilla* chiles,
I wondered why so many people
with yards, balconies, and windowsills
still purchased herbs and spices.
My garden beds were burgeoning
with Mexican oregano, *epazote*,
basil, chives, and mints.

Gary Paul Nabhan, *Coming Home to Eat*

PICK CUCUMBERS WHEN THEY'RE FIRM, rich green, and just to optimal size (depends on the variety). The bigger and yellower they get, the more watered down or bitter the flavor.

UNDER-WATERED CUCUMBER PLANTS will also produce bitter-tasting cucumbers, so be sure to water your cukes often and well.

Older cucumber plants often succumb to powdery mildew, a common fungal disease that looks like gray powder on leaves. Pull up and compost or discard affected plants.

You are also far less likely
to waste food
when you have
nurtured it from a
seed into a plant.

Darina Allen,
Grow Cook Nourish

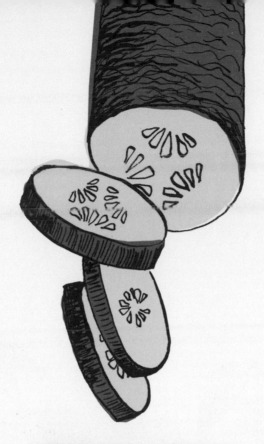

⎯ IN THE KITCHEN ⎯

Juice extra and overgrown cucumbers
and freeze in ice trays. Use the
refreshing cubes to flavor water
and summery cocktails.

Cut peppers from the plant using pruners or scissors to avoid snapping the stems.

All peppers – red, yellow, orange, purple, brown – start out green. Leaving the pepper to mature to its ripe color ensures that it will be as sweet or as hot as it can be.

ROASTED PEPPERS

Roasting brings out a pepper's sweetness and makes the skin easy to remove. It also softens the texture so you can easily purée peppers into a sauce or soup, or chop and add them to pasta or risotto.

1. Place whole peppers directly on a hot grill, no prep required.

2. Turn with tongs for a consistent char.

3. When blackened, move to a bowl and cover with a plate or plastic wrap until cool.

4. Rub off the charred skin.

Raw, grilled, or roasted peppers freeze well. Just halve, slice, or chop them, and freeze in bags.

SUCKERS ARE SIDE SHOOTS that grow on tomato plants between the main stem and branches in what's called the crotch. They will grow to become new branches that flower and fruit. Some gardeners swear by pruning suckers regularly, especially for indeterminate varieties, while others don't bother, and still others believe that pruning decreases photosynthesis. Try each method and see what works best for you.

> The plus side of the do-it-yourself experience is that the lessons learned that way tend to stick. I generally encourage learning by doing, in part because I've found my own mistakes so instructive.

Jeanne Nolan, *From the Ground Up*

For storage, most vegetables need to be clipped off the plant with up to an inch of the stem intact, which helps them retain moisture during storage, whether for two days or two months.

After being picked, **GREEN BEANS**
respire (release carbon dioxide)
at a faster rate than any
other vegetable, meaning
they spoil quickly. Wrap them
in plastic before placing in the fridge to
slow respiration and keep them
fresher longer.

Pick a tomato like a pro by gently lifting up on the fruit so that the stem breaks at a natural point called the knuckle, leaving a short piece of stem and the calyx (technically part of the flower, though it looks like little leaves) attached. This will help you avoid inadvertently bruising the tomato.

DON'T REFRIGERATE
YOUR TOMATOES —

it makes them mealy and flavorless.
If you can't eat or cook with them
within about a week of harvest,
preserve them by canning, freezing,
or dehydrating.

In terms of things
you can do to have
a better life,
picking berries
simply works.

Barbara Pleasant,
Homegrown Pantry

Stop yourself from picking blueberries as soon
as they turn blue. Instead, wait a few more days
until the berries feel slightly soft and separate from
the stems easily.

To stop the birds from picking the blueberries
before you can, cover your plants with bird netting.

◇◇

While tomatoes, peppers, and eggplant
love heat, too much heat and humidity
can prevent these plants from producing well.
You may see flowers simply drop from plants
without ever making fruit. Wait it out until
the heat wave subsides, and plants should
bounce back. If you typically have periods
above 90°F, plant heat-tolerant varieties.

◇◇

Tomatoes crack

when they get an influx of water after a dry spell and the fruit fills before the skin can catch up. Cracks make the fruit susceptible to pests and diseases, so harvest cracked tomatoes quickly. If this is a consistent problem, plant varieties labeled as crack resistant.

Before oregano flowers in summer,
cut the plant down to about 2 inches
from the ground. It'll produce another
similar harvest before first frost.
Oregano is easy to dry by hanging or
by placing on a screen or in a dehydrator.

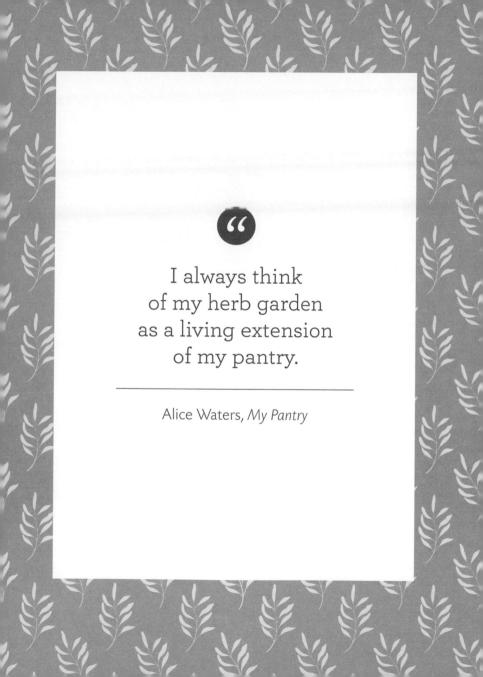

"

I always think
of my herb garden
as a living extension
of my pantry.

Alice Waters, *My Pantry*

Harvest broccoli

when the heads are tight
and green. Don't wait for them
to reach a certain size. If they
go too long, the heads will open
and begin to flower.

IF PREPPED CORRECTLY,
broccoli stalks are
edible and tasty. First peel them
to remove the tough skin,
then chop or slice them to use
alongside the florets.

Pick corn when the husks feel full and the silks are brown and starting to dry. Harvest early in the morning for the sweetest flavor.

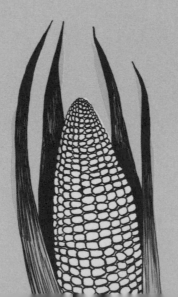
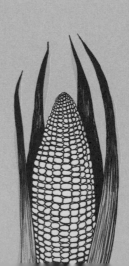

TO FREEZE CORN,
start by blanching the cobs
in boiling water for a few minutes.
Then remove the kernels
with a knife. Place cooled kernels
in a zip-top freezer bag, removing air
before freezing.

**IF ONE FRUIT ON
A MELON PLANT IS
RIPE, THE OTHERS
WILL FOLLOW SHORTLY.**
You can be sure that cantaloupe
and honeydew are ripe when
the rind changes from gray-green
to yellow-beige. Also, when ripe,
the stem attached to the fruit
may be cracked and should
detach easily from the vine.

TRY THE "THUMP" TEST

to see if a watermelon is ripe: when you tap it lightly, you should hear a thump instead of a ping. Test a few to get an ear for the difference.

CANTALOUPE is prone
to fast decay. To slow down this process,
dip a newly harvested melon in
hot water for a few minutes to kill any
mold and fungus, then dry
before storing in the refrigerator.

Melon rinds are a great addition
to your compost. They'll break down
quickly and contribute phosphorus
and potassium to the mix.

Pick eggplant

when the skin is tight and glossy. Dull-looking eggplant is past its prime and will have bitter-tasting seeds.

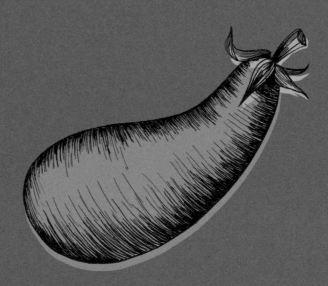

BABA GANOUSH

This easy-to-make Mediterranean dip with roasted eggplant and tahini (sesame seed paste) will convert even the most determined eggplant skeptic. Like hummus, it can be served as an appetizer, a side, or a spread on sandwiches or wraps.

1. Slice 1 medium-sized eggplant (or 2 to 3 smaller ones) and sprinkle with salt to soften. After 10 minutes, rinse and pat dry.

2. Cook on a hot grill 10 minutes, or roast at 450°F for 20 minutes, lightly browning both sides.

3. Remove the skin, if desired.

4. Purée the eggplant with 1 garlic clove, juice of 1 lemon, 2 tablespoons tahini, and a pinch of sea salt.

5. Top with chopped parsley, cilantro, basil, or mint. Serve at room temperature with pita or cucumber slices.

SUMMER

"

Do as little as possible
to an ingredient
when it's perfect and
at its peak.

Sean Brock, *Heritage*

SALTING EGGPLANT BEFORE COOKING
isn't necessary, but some feel it tones
down bitterness. Eggplant harvested at
its peak shouldn't taste bitter, but salting
also breaks down eggplant's spongy
texture, helping it better absorb flavors.

HOT-PEPPER VINEGAR

Simple hot-pepper vinegar is a ubiquitous condiment in the South. It adds zip to everything from barbecue to catfish to beans and greens.

1. Pack hot peppers into a clean pint jar.

2. Heat 1 cup vinegar with 1 tablespoon each sugar and salt, and bring to a boil.

3. Ladle vinegar over peppers and let the jar sit at room temperature for at least a week before using.

4. Refrigerate after opening.

SUMMER

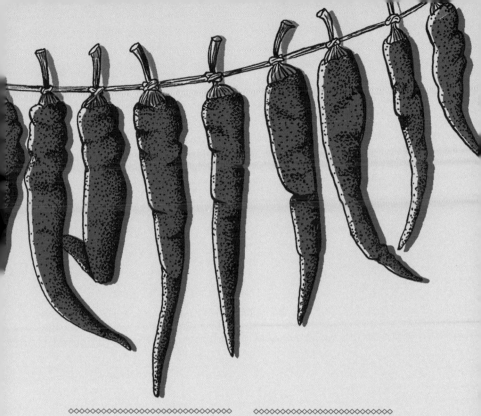

IN ARID CLIMATES,
dry hot peppers outdoors
on a screen, or make a
pretty pepper string. Use a
large needle to thread twine
through the tops of long,
skinny peppers, like cayenne.
Leave some space between
each pepper to allow for
airflow.

IN HUMID REGIONS,
dry peppers indoors,
or use a dehydrator in a
well-ventilated space.

◇◇

In a good year, a community or school garden,

or even your backyard garden,

can grow more than its members can eat.

Make a shared commitment

to donate any extra produce you won't

preserve to a local food bank.

◇◇

The bounty of fall
taught us how,
by investing ourselves —
our time, energy, and love —
we were able to fulfill
the promise of spring and
share our harvest with others.

Michelle Obama,
American Grown

When I found myself with a
garden, faced with a surplus
of cabbages and radishes,
sauerkraut beckoned me.
Our love affair endures.

Sandor Ellix Katz,
The Art of Fermentation

PLANT CABBAGES in late summer
for a fall harvest to make sauerkraut,
a great entrée to fermentation.
Up your game by also planting
daikon radishes to make kimchi,
the popular Korean ferment of cabbage,
daikon radish, garlic, and spices.

• •

In the process of **FERMENTATION**,
healthy bacteria break down chemicals,
primarily sugars, and help preserve food.
Eating fermented foods can promote a
healthy gut by cultivating beneficial
bacteria in the belly.

SUMMER

**MAKE HOMEGROWN
ZUCCHINI BREAD YEAR ROUND.**
Grate zucchini when fresh, squeeze out
some moisture, and freeze the right
amounts needed for your favorite
recipes in individual bags. Label clearly
with the recipe name. Yellow squash
works great for baking, too.

GAZPACHO

Traditional gazpacho is a perfect way to enjoy your summer yield. You can also play around with flavors and ingredients, such as swapping tomato for cantaloupe or watermelon and adding fresh herbs or some hot peppers.

1. Purée 2 pounds tomatoes, 1 bell pepper, 1 cucumber, ½ red onion, and 1 clove garlic.

2. Combine the purée with ¼ cup olive oil, 2 teaspoons wine vinegar, salt, and pepper.

3. Chill before serving.

SUMMER

BEET GREENS have a texture and flavor similar to chard's. After harvesting beets, lightly sauté the greens, or save them in the fridge or freezer to use later in soups.

• •

Many people don't like greens because they've only eaten overcooked ones. But greens, like **KALE, MUSTARD,** and **COLLARDS,** when lightly blanched for a few seconds, are delicious. Of course, you can also just sauté them.

"

Start eating kale because it's good for you, and you may end up eating it because it's good.

Ruth Page,
Ruth Page's Gardening Journal

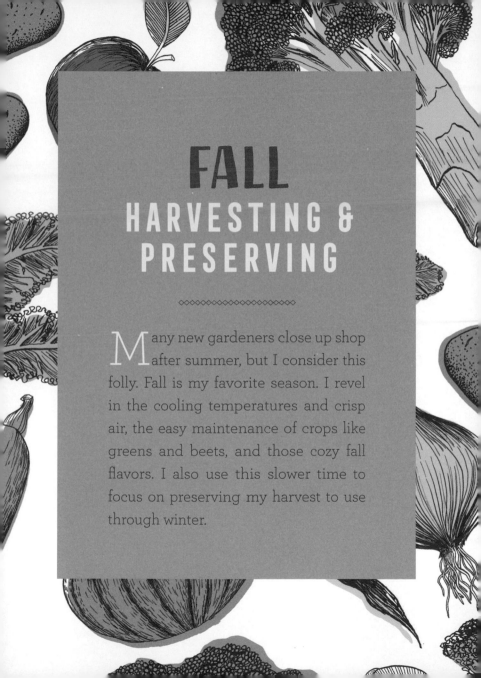

FALL
HARVESTING &
PRESERVING

◇◇◇◇◇◇◇◇◇◇◇◇◇◇◇◇

Many new gardeners close up shop after summer, but I consider this folly. Fall is my favorite season. I revel in the cooling temperatures and crisp air, the easy maintenance of crops like greens and beets, and those cozy fall flavors. I also use this slower time to focus on preserving my harvest to use through winter.

I remember my initial amazement when I learned that potatoes came from under the ground. I spent the harvest carving into just-dug potatoes with a pocketknife, drinking up the truffled aroma of the moist tubers mixed with earth and eating them raw, straight from the field.

Sean Brock, *Heritage*

Turn harvesting any underground crop,
particularly potatoes, into a game for kids,
like searching for buried treasure.

Harvest potatoes after the plant blooms and
the leaves start to turn yellow and die back.
Depending on your growing method, you can
dump containers out to harvest or dig for the potatoes
in the bed by hand. You can also dig with a garden fork,
but you risk spearing some spuds.

Cure potatoes for about a week
in a dry spot away from the sun.
Cover them with a towel to block light,
which causes potato skin to turn green.
Store them in a ventilated box or bag in the
coolest place you can find, but don't keep
them in the refrigerator, which is too cold and
will cause potatoes to darken when cooked.

Potatoes aren't roots; they're swollen stems (known as "stem tubers"), which is why they sprout. Roots don't sprout.

**DON'T STORE VEGETABLES
WITH APPLES —**
apples give off ethylene gas,
which causes nearby produce
to decay more quickly
and even causes onions to sprout.

Before storing pumpkins
or winter squash,
you can dip them in a
diluted bleach solution —
1 PART BLEACH TO 10 PARTS WATER —
to remove any fungus or bacteria
that would hasten rotting.

A fun trick for storing onions and garlic:

Drop them one by one in a pantyhose leg, tying a knot between each to separate them, and hang. The fine hose mesh will help maintain good airflow and keep the bulbs dry. When you want an onion, simply snip off the hose below the next knot.

Pantyhose aren't a one-trick pony in gardening. Wrap them around melons and winter squash as they grow on the vine to shield the expanding fruit from squirrels and other nibblers.

You can also cut pantyhose into strips to use as ties for tomatoes. The soft, stretchy material supports without cutting into the tender tomato stems.

Plant lettuce of different hues and
textures in stripes or blocks
to create an edible quilt of color.

'Bright Lights' Swiss chard
is a beautiful choice for cool-season containers,
with stems that grow in a rainbow of colors from
yellow and orange to pink, red, and white.

Swiss chard seems like a cross between
spinach and beets because it's related to both —
the green tops look and taste like spinach
while the stems have a bright color and earthy flavor
like beets. Grow and harvest it like spinach.

Pick all your tomatoes before the first frost.
Those partially ripened will
continue coloring up indoors.
Place green tomatoes in a cardboard box
between layers of newspaper
along with a banana or apple,
which will release ethylene gas and
speed up the ripening process.

TO PEEL TOMATOES FOR CANNING,
drop them whole in boiling water for
about 30 seconds, then remove the peel
with a sharp knife when the tomato
is cool enough to touch.

You can freeze whole,
UNPEELED TOMATOES
in freezer bags or
quarter them and freeze.
After letting them thaw,
remove the peel using a knife
while holding the fruits
under warm water.

Growing and preserving
at least some of your own food
will also make you feel
more secure in a wild and
ever-changing world.
News of war, sickness, and
economic collapse loses some
of its punch when you are
sitting in the shade with a
basket of snap beans in your lap
or lingering in the kitchen to
hear the last canning lids pop.

Barbara Pleasant, *Homegrown Pantry*

Chinese cabbage

(napa is a popular type) and bok choy (or pak choi) are Asian types of cabbage with looser heads and thick, succulent stalks. They mature more quickly than heading cabbages, making them ideal for fall growing.

Collards are a cabbage-family crop grown widely in the South (they were even named the state vegetable of South Carolina), but they can be grown anywhere. Plant them in fall and grow throughout winter and on into next summer. They're more heat tolerant than their cabbage cousins, meaning the tender, nutritious greens can be harvested nearly year round.

Cold-loving Brussels sprouts

form handfuls of mini cabbages along a thick stalk.

Harvest Brussels sprouts when about 1 inch in size and still tight, before they begin to open. Remove the leaf below each bud in order to more easily snap or cut off the mini cabbages.

Kale needs to be covered
during a hard freeze,
but it tolerates frost very well.
In fact, like many cool-weather crops,
it tastes better after a little frost.
Lower-growing varieties of kale
tolerate frost better than tall varieties.

◇◇

Small, young kale leaves are the most tender
and don't need the center ribs removed before eating,
making them perfect for salads.

KALE CHIPS

Kale surprises and delights as a crisp chip. Make your own in a dehydrator or in the oven, playing around with spices to get a taste you love.

1. Remove stems, and tear leaves into smaller pieces.

2. Use your hands to work a little olive oil into the kale; a half tablespoon is plenty for 6 cups kale.

3. Add a dash of sea salt and, if desired, spices like garlic powder and cayenne.

4. Dry until crisp: 3 to 4 hours on trays in a dehydrator at 125°F, or about 20 minutes on a parchment-lined cookie sheet in a 250°F oven.

BROCCOLI RABE'S edible flower heads inspired its name, but the plant is actually more closely related to turnips than broccoli, which is evidenced by its leaves. Broccoli rabe grows faster than its namesake and can tolerate a little frost, making it a good choice if you've had trouble with broccoli's temperature sensitivity. You may hear it called just *rabe* or *rapini*, which can refer to any cabbage-family plant allowed to bolt and eaten in its entirety — leaves, flower head, and all.

PURPLE VARIETIES of vegetables, such as cabbage, cauliflower, snap beans, and carrots, lose much of their color when cooked, because the anthocyanins making the pretty purple hue decompose quickly when exposed to heat. Add an acid such as lemon juice or vinegar when cooking to help retain some of the color.

BECOME SELF-SUFFICIENT IN GARLIC.

Start in fall with quality seed garlic ordered from a seed company. Divide bulbs into individual cloves, and plant with pointed ends up. By harvest time in summer, each clove will have developed into a new full bulb.

CHOOSE FROM THREE KINDS OF GARLIC:

Hardneck is the most winter hardy with a strong central stem.

Softneck has a stronger flavor and softer stems that can be braided.

Elephant produces fewer, larger cloves with milder flavor.

Rather than peeling a bunch of
GARLIC CLOVES one by one,
try this: Drop them in boiling water
for 30 seconds, then quickly cool them
over ice. The peelings will be easy
to remove or practically
remove themselves.

Many medicinal plants
have entered into the
household via the
kitchen door, ushered in by
the Mistress of Spices,
their healing spirits
camouflaged in
culinary garb.

Rosemary Gladstar,
Rosemary's Gladstar's Medicinal Herbs

AROMATIC ROSEMARY OPENS AIRWAYS.

Heat a cup of water, add lemon juice, honey, and a sprig of
rosemary, and breathe deeply before each sip to soothe sinuses.

Let dill plants flower and allow the seeds
to turn brown. Then cut the seed heads
and continue drying them in a paper bag.
Many seeds will drop into the bag, and
the rest should be easy to remove from the
flower. Store dill seed in airtight containers.

FRIED SAGE LEAVES

Frying fresh sage leaves in oil subdues the herb's rich, earthy flavor. The crunchy sage leaves perfectly complement smooth vegetable soups and pastas such as gnocchi.

1. Harvest a bunch of garden sage and pinch off individual leaves.

2. Heat ¼ cup olive oil in a small skillet over medium-high heat.

3. Fry a few leaves at a time in oil for 2 to 3 seconds until crisp, then transfer with a fork to a paper towel. Sprinkle just-fried leaves with a little sea salt.

4. Use fried leaves to top a savory winter soup, like potato or pumpkin, or eat as a snack.

HARVEST BEETS when they're 2 inches wide, give or take a half inch. Larger beets will have a woody texture and less flavor.

After harvest, **gently wash soil off beets**, but don't scrub them, which can remove too much skin. Cut off all but an inch of the tops, and leave the taproot intact to avoid the "bleeding" juices. **Golden beets** are milder in flavor as well as color and won't "bleed" as much dye-like juice as scarlet beets when cut and cooked.

BEETS, CHARD, AND SPINACH, as well as the pseudo-grains amaranth and quinoa, come from the same plant family, named for **amaranth.** Quinoa and amaranth are grown for their edible seeds but are not cereal grains (from grasses).

Cabbage-family plants

are sometimes called "cole" crops, from the Latin word *caulis*, meaning stalk or stem. But it's the leaves that destructive **cabbage worms and loopers** are after.

If your leaves look like lace, look closely for green caterpillars on all parts of the plant and pick them off by hand.

> **"**
>
> The cabbage loopers are the paratroopers of the vegetable patch: their eggs are dropped on the cole crops by troop transports disguised as innocuous white butterflies.

Michael Pollan,
Second Nature: A Gardener's Education

> "

I realize today as I wash the last of the just-dug carrots in the sink — cleaning up even the littlest ones because the crop was so bad this year — that what this is all really about is using up, making do, cutting down, even more than it's about eating locally.... It is my meditation, my learning, my caring for each thing the earth has produced as if my life depends on it, because of course, in a larger sense, it does.

Joan Dye Gussow,
This Organic Life: Confessions of a Suburban Homesteader

DIG UP FALL-GROWN CARROTS

before the ground freezes.
Clip the green tops off, leaving about an
inch of stem, to prolong storage life.

MAKE YOUR OWN POWDERED GREENS
for smoothies by dehydrating leftover
kale, mustard greens, carrot tops,
or beet tops, grinding them into
a powder in a blender or with mortar
and pestle, and storing in an airtight jar
or zip-top bag.

SAVE SCRAPS, like onion ends, carrot peels, broccoli stems, celery ends, mushroom stems, extra herbs, and more, for making your own vegetable broth. Keep scraps in a freezer bag until you're ready, then simmer the veggies in water on the stove or in a slow cooker for a couple of hours. Strain, cool, and store in the fridge or freezer. Your homemade broth will infuse cozy soups and stews with fresh-from-the-garden flavor all winter long.

Pumpkins and large winter squash growing all season with one side resting on the ground may develop a bit lopsided. Avoid this by turning the fruit every so often, being careful not to damage the stem.

The rind of most winter squash varieties is too tough to eat, but Delicata is a lovely, more tender variety that can be sliced, seeded, roasted, and eaten — rind and all.

ROASTED SQUASH SEEDS

When cooking fall squash or pumpkins, don't toss the seeds. Instead, roast them for a simple snack or salad topping.

1. Collect the seeds and rinse off the pulp.

2. Toss the seeds with a little olive oil and salt.

3. Spread them on a baking sheet and roast at about 400°F for 20 minutes.

Beans and peas

make good crops for first-time seed
savers, in part because the seeds are
so large. Just let the pods dry on the
plant, then harvest the seeds inside,
and store until next year.

If you save seeds from this year's harvest,
be sure they're completely dry before storing.
Try the snap test to be sure — a dry seed will
snap or shatter, not bend, under stress.

Store saved seeds in a dry place without
temperature fluctuations or direct sunlight.
You can store in the refrigerator or freezer
but only in airtight containers because the
humidity could cause rot or sprouting.

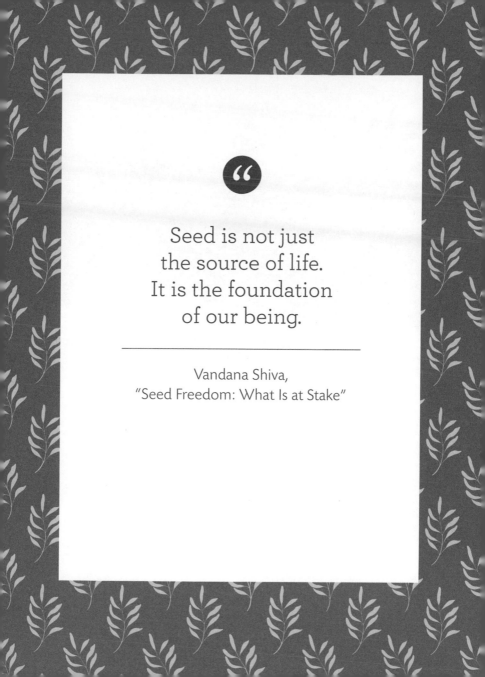

Seed is not just
the source of life.
It is the foundation
of our being.

Vandana Shiva,
"Seed Freedom: What Is at Stake"

PARSNIPS AND LEEKS are two vegetable plants that
will live through winter, even in cold climates. A thick layer of
mulch helps keep them happy through winter and harvestable
come spring.

Cut back asparagus ferns in
fall when they are brown and dry.
Amend the soil with compost,
then cover it with straw mulch
to protect the plants through winter.

Clean up spent garden vegetables after the season has waned — don't leave them in your garden. There are living things still on your plants, including pest eggs, fungus, and bacteria that can overwinter and cause problems next year. Toss or compost the plants instead.

Many gardeners won't compost
the roots of any plants in the
cabbage family to avoid spreading
common soilborne diseases.

RETHINK FALL LEAVES ON YOUR LAWN.

Rather than a nuisance, they're a valuable crop ready to harvest and feed your soil. Shred them first with a leaf shredder or lawnmower, then use as mulch for winter insulation, to add carbon to compost, or to loosen the soil and feed earthworms and microbes in garden beds.

Grow cover crops

(also called green manures) — such as peas, winter rye, and buckwheat — during downtimes, including winter, to enrich soil that would otherwise be bare. Rather than harvesting them for food, cut these crops back and work them into the soil as fertilizer.

That promise,
the return every spring
of earth's first freshness,
would never be kept
if not for the frosts and rots
and ripe deaths of fall.

Michael Pollan,
Second Nature: A Gardener's Education

YEAR-ROUND GARDENING IS A NOBLE GOAL,

and it can be rewarding to grow a few plants indoors and out-doors through winter. But there's also something to be said for winter rest and restoration, both for the gardener and the garden.

ACKNOWLEDGMENTS

I feel so fortunate to have been raised by parents and grandparents who would never consider themselves makers or DIYers, just responsible humans. If self-reliance is hereditary, I happily accept this trait. If it's learned, I'm obliged to have you as teachers.

Thanks to my mom, Sharon, who taught me that a woman's place is anywhere she wants to be, including the kitchen and the garden, and my dad, Floyd, who, as punishment after a fit of teenage rebellion, unwittingly taught me to work out my problems with a shovel and a pile of cow manure. The angst faded, but my respect for you, and for compost, endures.

I also thank my grandfather, Floyd Sr., for always planting at least a few okra and tomato plants, no matter what, and my grandmother, Patricia, for introducing me to preserving at a young age. No one's green beans are better than yours.

A heartfelt thank-you goes to my sister, Bonnie, for leading the way by example and encouragement and for giving thoughtful notes and advice.

I am also fortunate to have two parents by marriage, Mike and Deb, with green thumbs, curious minds, and an active kitchen. Someday, I will grow rhubarb for you.

I couldn't write a book about vegetables without acknowledging Lois Chaplin, who taught me so much in two years that she could've granted me a degree. Lois, when it comes to vegetable gardening wisdom, you are the sage.

Thanks to everyone at Storey Publishing for their help and support. To Carleen, for helping shape the book and suggesting the addition of quotes. Spending a winter voraciously reading my favorite garden and food authors was a luxury I wouldn't mind repeating. To Hannah, my editor, for bringing it all together. We've always been on the same page. To the art department for these beautiful pages and illustrator Harriet Popham for making gardening look as fun and full of color as I've found it to be. And to Alee and the PR team for promoting the book and introducing me to fellow Storey author Niki Jabbour, a truly generous soul and new friend.

And finally, I must thank Derek. I'm so grateful for that 60-day return policy. You and Rufus are the best family I could imagine. Thank you for building all the things.

METRIC CONVERSION CHARTS

VOLUME

US	Metric
1 teaspoon	5 milliliters
1 tablespoon	15 milliliters
¼ cup	60 milliliters
½ cup	120 milliliters
1 cup	240 milliliters

LENGTH

To convert	to	multiply
inches	millimeters	inches by 25.4
inches	centimeters	inches by 2.54
inches	meters	inches by 0.0254
feet	meters	feet by 0.3048

INDEX